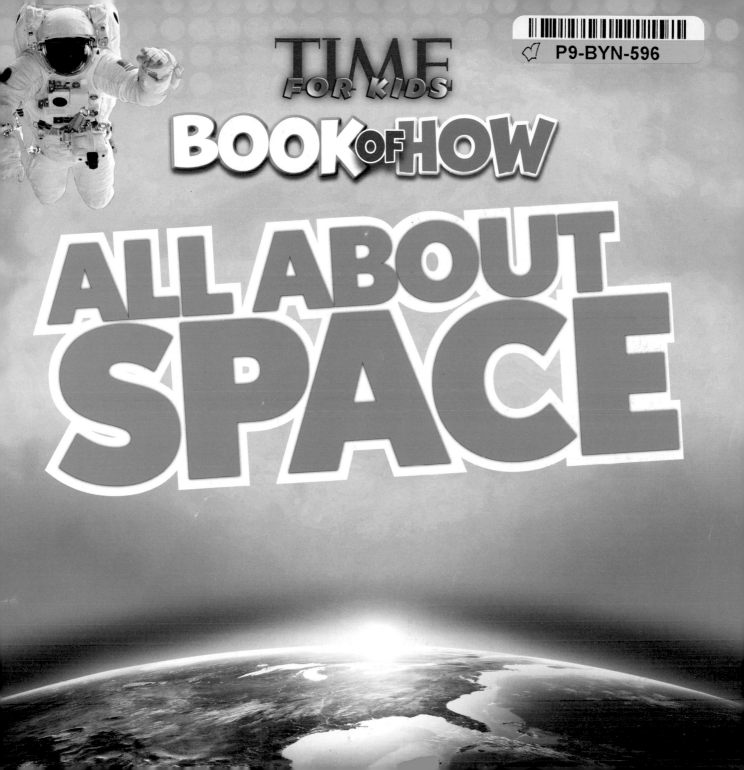

TIME
FOR KIDS
BOOK OF HOW

ALL ABOUT SPACE

TIME FOR KIDS

Managing Editor, TIME FOR KIDS: Nellie Gonzalez Cutler
Editor, Time Learning Ventures: Jonathan Rosenbloom

Book Packager: R studio T, New York
Art Direction/Design: Raúl Rodriguez and Rebecca Tachna
Writer: Curtis Slepian
Illustrator: Felipe Galindo
Photo Researcher: Elizabeth Vezzulla
Special Thanks to: Harry Chamberlain, Anne Jewell, Zane Martin, Donna Moxley Scarborough, Neil Soderstrom, Turkey Hill Dairy

BOOKWORKS INC.

REDESIGN BY DOWNTOWN BOOKWORKS, INC.
Project Manager: Sara DiSalvo

COVER DESIGN BY SYMBOLOGY CREATIVE
Designer: Mark Wainwright

Time
HOME ENTERTAINMENT

TIME HOME ENTERTAINMENT
Publisher Jim Childs
Vice President and Associate Publisher Margot Schupf
Vice President, Finance Vandana Patel
Executive Director, Marketing Services Carol Pittard
Executive Director, Business Development Suzanne Albert
Executive Director, Marketing Susan Hettleman
Publishing Director Megan Pearlman
Associate Director of Publicity Courtney Greenhalgh
Assistant General Counsel Simone Procas
Assistant Director, Special Sales Ilene Schreider
Senior Marketing Manager, Sales Marketing Danielle Costa
Associate Production Manager Amy Mangus
Associate Prepress Manager Alex Voznesenskiy
Associate Project Manager Stephanie Braga

Editorial Director Stephen Koepp
Senior Editor Roe D'Angelo
Editors Katie McHugh Malm, Jonathan White
Copy Chief Rina Bander
Design Manager Anne-Michelle Gallero
Editorial Operations Gina Scauzillo
Editorial Assistant Courtney Mifsud

Special Thanks to: Katherine Barnet, Brad Beatson, Jeremy Biloon, Susan Chodakiewicz, Rose Cirrincione, Assu Etsubneh, Mariana Evans, Christine Font, Hillary Hirsch, David Kahn, Jean Kennedy, Kimberly Marshall, Nina Mistry, Dave Rozzelle, Matthew Ryan, Ricardo Santiago, Divyam Shrivastava, Adriana Tierno

Contents of this book previously appeared in Time For Kids Big Book of HOW.

For information on TIME For Kids magazine for the classroom or home, go to WWW.TFKCLASSROOM.COM or call 1-800-777-8600.

For subscriptions to Sports Illustrated Kids, go to www.sikids.com or call 1-800-889-6007.

Published by TIME For Kids Books
an imprint of Time Home Entertainment Inc.
1271 Avenue of the Americas
New York, New York 10020

ISBN 10: 1-61893-361-2
ISBN 13: 978-1-61893-361-4

"TIME For Kids" is a trademark of Time Inc.

We welcome your comments and suggestions about TIME For Kids Books.
Please write to us at:
TIME For Kids Books
Attention: Book Editors
PO Box 11016
Des Moines, IA 50336-1016

If you would like to order any of our hardcover Collector's Edition books, please call us at 800-327-6388. (Monday through Friday, 7:00 a.m.– 8:00 p.m. or Saturday, 7:00 a.m.– 6:00 p.m. Central Time).

1 QGT 14

Contents

Chapter 1: Space

How Can We Protect Earth from Big Space Rocks? 4
How Will the Juno Probe Uncover Jupiter's Secrets? 6
How Do Astronauts Train? 8
How Does the Sun Stay Hot? 10
How Do We Know If There's Another Earth Out There? 12
How to Build a Planetarium 14
How to Launch a Rocket 16

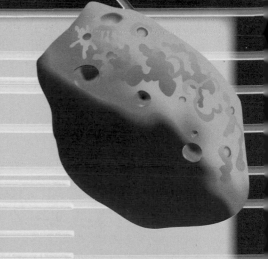

Chapter 2: Buildings

How Were the Egyptian Pyramids Built? 18
How Was Mount Rushmore Built? 20
How Does the Panama Canal Work? 22
How Was a Bridge Built Across the Colorado River? 24
How to Build a Spaghetti Bridge 26
How to Build a Pyramid 28

Chapter 3: Transportation

How Do Submarines Work? 30
How Does a Hybrid Car Work? 32
How Are Tunnels Dug? 34
How Does a Maglev Train Work? 36
How Does a Toilet Flush Away Waste? 38
How to Make a Baking-Soda Boat 40
How to Make a Paper Airplane 42

Glossary 44
Photo Credits 46
Index 47

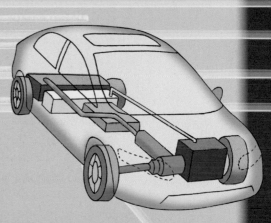

HOW Can We Protect Earth from Big Space Rocks?

Every day, 100 tons of asteroids and comets land on the surface of Earth. Almost all of these pieces are too tiny to cause harm. But much larger rocks have struck Earth. Millions of years ago, a rock about a mile and a half wide and weighing 10 billion tons hit what is now Manson, Illinois. It created a crater three miles deep and about 18 miles wide. Glaciers smoothed over the crater, so it's no longer visible. About 65 million years ago, a huge comet hit near Mexico, leaving a crater 110 miles across. Its blast may have wiped out the dinosaurs.

Can we get hit again by a large meteor or asteroid? According to scientists, about 320,000 asteroids larger than 300 feet across orbit within our solar system. If any one of them hit Earth, it would be a disaster. Scientists think that none of those rocks will collide with our planet during the next few hundred thousand years. But if one of them did head toward Earth, how could we avoid getting hit? Scientists are coming up with plans to keep Earth safe.

Early Warning: To keep Earth safe from comets and asteroids, scientists first have to pinpoint where the rocks are. NASA's Near Earth Object Program is locating and tracking at least 90 percent of space rocks larger than 450 feet in our solar system.

Bad Breakup: Scientists wouldn't blast a space rock to pieces with a nuclear missile. Those pieces could hit Earth and cause just as much damage. But a nuclear blast set off near a small rock might completely vaporize it.

People have always kept their eyes on the skies. Thanks to powerful telescopes, space probes, and brave astronauts, our knowledge of heavenly bodies is at an all-time high.

Nudge, Nudge: Setting off a nuclear weapon high above the surface of a large space rock would heat its surface. That would make the rock move slightly in the opposite direction, changing its speed and causing it to miss Earth.

Hot Spot: Instead of using a nuclear blast to nudge the space object, laser beams from a spacecraft would do the trick.

Mutual Attraction: A large unmanned spacecraft could be put in orbit around a space rock. The gravity of both objects would attract each other. This would change the path of the space rock enough to avoid Earth.

Catching Rays: One bright idea is to place large solar sails on the space object. Rays from the sun would push against the surface of the sails and slowly redirect the object away from Earth.

Rocking Russia

On June 30, 1908, a huge explosion took place in Tunguska, a remote part of Russia. The blast knocked down trees for 20 miles. People living 250 miles from the explosion saw a huge fireball that rose 12 miles in the sky. An area of several hundred square miles was scorched. The sound of the blast was heard 500 miles away.

Scientists think the explosion was caused by a comet or an asteroid about 500 feet wide and weighing 7 million tons. As the object sped through Earth's atmosphere, it heated up and exploded about five miles above the ground. No fragments were left behind. Fortunately, the object burst over an unpopulated area.

HOW Will the Juno Probe Uncover Jupiter's Secrets?

Jupiter is the largest planet in the solar system, and it holds some big secrets. Scientists don't know for sure what's going on under the gas giant's 621-mile-thick atmosphere. That may change in 2016, when the unmanned Juno spacecraft is scheduled to reach Jupiter after traveling five years. Juno will come within 3,000 miles of Jupiter's cloud tops—which, in space terms, is very close. For one year, Juno will send back information during 33 orbits of the planet, including the first clear pictures of the planet's poles.

NASA scientists put together the Juno spacecraft. They hope it will help reveal the history of Jupiter and the solar system.

The spacecraft will get its power from solar panels. They will stretch out more than 66 feet to gather sunlight that's 25 times weaker than light striking Earth.

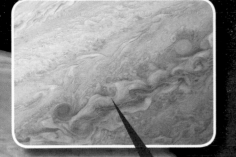

Fact File: Jupiter

Jupiter is the largest planet in the solar system. Covered by swirling clouds, the planet is made mostly of hydrogen and helium in the forms of gas and liquid. Here are more facts about the fifth planet from the sun:

Diameter: 88,650 miles (11 times greater than Earth's diameter)
Average distance from the sun: 483,682,810 miles
Average distance from Earth: 391,463,851 miles
Average surface temperature: −238°F
Surface gravity: 2.53 times that of Earth's
Length of day: 9.93 hours
Length of year: 11.87 Earth years
Number of moons: 62
Number of rings: 3

Instruments aboard the craft will record data that might explain what Jupiter's clouds are made of, how thick they are, how they move, and why winds blow them at speeds up to 372 miles per hour.

Jupiter

Juno will map Jupiter's powerful magnetic field (shown here), which spreads far out into space. This information may offer clues about what the planet's core is made of.

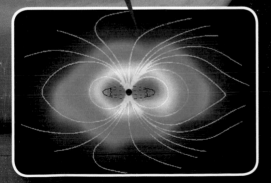

The Missing Belt

The atmosphere of Jupiter is made up of light-colored layers of clouds called bands and dark layers called belts. These layers last for many years. But recently, a giant belt suddenly disappeared, and no one knew why. Then, months later, the belt began to reappear. Experts think that the belt had just been covered by white clouds driven by powerful winds. Now it seems the white clouds are drifting away to reveal the darker belt beneath.

HOW Do Astronauts Train?

Since the early days of space exploration, astronauts have landed on the moon, walked in space, performed experiments on the space shuttle, and spent time on the International Space Station.

Here's a look at some of the training astronauts get at the Lyndon B. Johnson Space Center, in Houston, Texas. Some of these astronauts may one day return to the moon—or blast off for Mars.

FACTOID

How do you become an astronaut? Here are some requirements:

● An astronaut must be a college graduate, with a major in technology, math, or other science fields.

● Many astronauts are pilots in the military, but civilians who have never flown can be astronauts too. These astronauts are called mission specialists, and they can be engineers, scientists, doctors, or researchers.

● An astronaut must be at least at least 4 feet 10½ inches tall and no more than 6 feet 4 inches tall.

Astronauts-in-training learn aircraft safety, including how to eject and parachute from a plane. They also undergo flight training. Space pilots have learned to fly aircraft built to work like the space shuttle.

Astronauts train for hours in a huge tank of water, which gives the feel of weightlessness. They do tasks in the water that they will do in zero gravity during spaceflight. One tank, the Neutral Buoyancy Laboratory, is 200 feet long and 40 feet deep. It's the largest indoor pool in the world.

To experience weightlessness, astronauts ride in airplanes that go high up and then dive. For 30 seconds during each dive, astronauts float around the cabin in zero-gravity conditions.

Candidates receive survival training. They are taught how to stay alive if their craft lands in the ocean or in a forest. They experience tough challenges so they will know what to do in a real situation.

A crew of astronauts practice living and working in mockups—exact copies of the spacecraft they'll fly. They also train in simulators that reproduce the events of a mission. Trainers give the crew problems to solve or put them in emergency situations to overcome.

The people on the ground who give information and instructions to astronauts during missions are called the flight-control team. An astronaut crew practices an upcoming mission with a particular flight-control team. That way, the actual flight will run smoothly.

HOW Does the Sun Stay Hot?

The temperature of the sun's surface is about 10,000°F. At its core, the sun is more than 27,000,000°F. The ancient Greeks believed the sun's heat came from a huge lump of coal that burned at its center. In the 1800s, some scientists thought the sun was filled with erupting volcanoes. Others believed the sun got hot from millions of meteorites striking it.

The sun started out as a massive ball of gas and dust. About 4.5 billion years ago, gravity squeezed together the particles so tightly that heat was produced—and the sun was born. But how does it continue to burn? Inside the sun, the intense heat at its birth started a process called nuclear fusion. Nuclear fusion happens when hydrogen atoms in the sun's core combine, or fuse, to form the element helium. This releases energy, which reaches Earth (93 million miles away) mostly in the form of light and heat. The sun has plenty of hydrogen, so it should keep us warm for about 5 billion more years.

Corona: The top layer of very hot gases stretches millions of miles into space.

Core: The center takes up only 2% of the sun's space, but holds 60% of its mass. Here, immense heat and pressure slam together parts of hydrogen atoms. The atoms fuse into helium atoms, releasing almost all the energy that keeps the sun shining.

Radiative Zone: The energy from the core rises in the form of particles called photons (*foh*-tahnz). Here, the energy of the photons is absorbed by various atoms. Those atoms then give off more energy. This way, energy slowly rises to the convective zone.

Convective Zone: In this layer, energy heats currents of gas, which rise to the surface of the sun. As the energy is released at the surface, the gas cools and falls back down.

Photosphere: This 200-mile- thick layer of swirling gas is the surface of the sun. The light that we see comes from this layer.

Chromosphere: From here, huge jets and sheets of hot gases rise above the surface of the sun and fall back.

Sun Safety

Sunlight is the reason there's life on Earth. But sunlight's ultraviolet (UV) rays can also give you a sunburn. Follow these tips to keep your skin safe during the day.

○ Stay in the shade, especially between 10 a.m. and 4 p.m., when the sun's rays are strongest.

○ Whenever you're out in the sun, even for a short walk, wear sunscreen with at least a 30 SPF rating. Use it year-round, not just in the summer.

○ When you're outside, cover up. Wear clothes that sunlight can't go through. Place a hand inside the clothes: If you can see your hand, the cloth isn't thick enough.

○ Protect your eyes. Wear sunglasses with labels that say the glasses have 100% UV protection. Wear a wide-brim hat that shades your eyes, ears, and face.

○ Don't forget your lips: Apply a lip balm that has an SPF of at least 15.

HOW Do We Know if There's Another Earth Out There?

It took observers thousands of years to discover all the planets in our solar system. But no one knew if any planets circled other stars—until 1995. That's when the first exoplanets were found. An exoplanet is a planet that orbits a star other than our own star, the sun. Since then, nearly 2,000 more exoplanets have been confirmed.

Could there be life on one of these exoplanets? The answer so far is maybe. Astronomers may have found one Earth-sized planet in a star's "Goldilocks zone." In this zone, things are not too hot, not too cold, but just right for life. Scientists are questioning whether this planet could harbor life. In the meantime, they keep looking. There are so many stars out there, there must be warm, watery Earth-like worlds orbiting some of them. And perhaps there is Earth-like life on one of those worlds.

Goldilocks Worlds: Where Things Are Just Right for Life

SOLAR SYSTEM

Habitable (Goldilocks) zone

The hot zone

Too Close: If a planet gets too close to a star, the heat can make all its water boil off, as happened to Mercury. The star can also warm a planet's surface to deadly temperatures, which was the fate of Venus.

FACTOID

Earth is just the right distance from the sun to support life. If it were 5 percent closer, all the water on Earth would have boiled away. If it were 15 percent farther away, all the water would be frozen.

Exo-llent Search!

For most of human history, we've known only about the planets that circle our sun. In the past 20 years, scientists have found 1,732 other planets orbiting distant stars. Most are giants compared with Earth. But new ways of searching are making it easier to find smaller ones—the kind where life may exist.

Exoplanets Discovered

Pre-2000 **32**

2000-09 **391**

2010-present **1,309**

Total: **1,732** *

* As of June 2014

Source: NASA

The Artist's Eye: This Earth-like world does not exist, but similar ones are probably out there.

STAR

The cold zone

Too Far: Space is a cold place. A planet doesn't have to be far from its sun to become frigid and have its water freeze solid. Atmosphere holds in heat, and Mars might have been a living world today if it had kept its atmosphere.

Just Right: Earth exists in the livable (Goldilocks) zone, where plenty of liquid water can be present. There may be different forms of life on other planets that orbit in a Goldilocks zone.

HOW to Build a Planetarium

The best way to see the Milky Way is to gaze up at the sky on a cloudless night. The next best way is to go to a planetarium. A planetarium is a theater where heavenly bodies are projected onto a dome-shaped screen. The device that projects the stars and planets is also called a planetarium. The first modern planetarium was built in 1924. It was a projector that shined lights through hundreds of tiny holes onto a wall to stand for stars.

Planetariums now use computers and high-tech projectors to show the positions of the stars and planets on any given night—past, present, and future. Many planetariums also have digital projection systems that can take viewers on a tour of the planets, show the birth of the solar system, and much more. Put on your own star show by making an out-of-this-world planetarium.

What You Need

- Empty cereal box
- Several 3-inch-by-5-inch index cards
- Pencil
- Flashlight
- Tape
- Scissors

What to Do

1 Cut out a rectangle in the underside of the cereal box. Make it a bit smaller than the index cards. The top of the box should be open.

2 Use the pencil to punch holes in an index card in the configuration of a constellation. Two constellations are drawn to help get you started (see "Constellations"). You can find other constellations online or in a reference book.

FACTOID

The earliest type of planetarium was a mechanical device called an orrery (or-er-ree). It rotated and revolved small globes that represented the sun and planets.

3 Tape the index card over the bottom of the cereal box.

4 Turn off the lights—the room should be dark. Stand a few feet from a blank wall. Hold the cereal box so the end with the index card is pointed toward the wall. Through the open end, shine the flashlight inside the cereal box at a 45 degree angle.

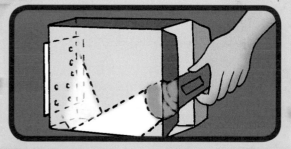

5 View the stars shining brightly on your wall. Make other index cards with constellations to create new star shows.

Constellations

In ancient times, people looked at the night sky and noticed groups of stars. When they imagined lines connecting these stars, it looked like people, animals, or objects. These clusters of stars are called constellations. Below are two of the 88 recognized constellations. Use these pictures to create index cards for your planetarium. Don't forget to label each constellation you make.

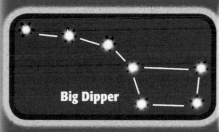

Big Dipper

Orion

FACTOID

The Hayden Sphere, in New York City, uses a one-of-a-kind high-definition projector and a powerful virtual reality simulator to create amazing, realistic shows. You can see programs that take you on a journey to a star, show cosmic collisions, and search for life in the universe.

HOW to Launch a Rocket

The first rockets ever launched were fireworks, set off in China more than a thousand years ago. The fireworks used the power of gun powder to take off. It wasn't until the mid-1900s that people began to build rockets to travel into space.

A space rocket needs a lot of power to lift off and escape Earth's gravity. The power comes from huge engines that burn tons of liquid fuel—often a combination of liquid oxygen and liquid hydrogen. As the gases push out the bottom of the rocket, the ship rises. But you can launch a rocket with something as simple as air power.

FACTOID

In 1926, American scientist Robert Goddard launched the first liquid-fueled rocket. Thanks to his work and that of others, rockets now send astronauts, satellites, and probes into space.

What You Need

- A plastic tennis-ball can with lid or a plastic soda bottle with cap
- Three different types of soda straws: jumbo, super jumbo, and flexible
- Large pencil
- Scissors
- Tape
- Paper

What to Do

1 Poke a hole in the lid of the plastic can or bottle with a large pencil or the pointed end of a pair of scissors. (Ask an adult for help.)

2 Cut the end of the flex straw on an angle. Push it through the hole in the lid or cap. The straw should fit snugly. Put the lid back on.

3 Stick a jumbo straw into the end of the flex straw. Tape it in place.

4 Make a rocket by folding over a half-inch of the end of a super-jumbo straw. (These straws can be found at a place that sells milk shakes.) Tape down the end.

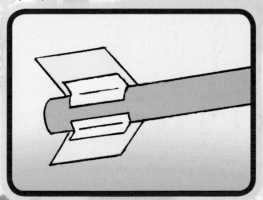

5 Make fins from paper to help your rocket fly straight. Tape on two or three paper fins to your super-jumbo straw.

6 Slide the super-jumbo straw over the jumbo launcher straw. Aim and give the can or bottle a sharp squeeze. Watch it blast off.

Why It Works

Air pressure, not burning gases, makes your rocket take off. When you squeeze the can or bottle, the air inside the straw is compressed into a smaller space. This causes the pressure in the container to increase. To release the pressure, air rushes out the open end of the straw, causing it to fly up and away—just like a real rocket.

FACTOID

When a rocket reaches a height of 150 miles, it must reach a speed of nearly five miles per second to orbit Earth. If the rocket moves at a speed of seven miles per second or faster, it will reach escape velocity and head into outer space.

HOW Were the Egyptian Pyramids Built?

The first pyramid was built in Egypt about 4,000 years ago. Pyramids were tombs for the kings of Egypt, called pharaohs. Hundreds of pyramids were built, and more than 100 still survive. The most famous are in Giza, outside of Cairo, the capital of Egypt.

It took thousands of people and a great deal of skill to build the pyramids. A small town was constructed near the pyramid site to house all workers and officials in charge, as well as the people who supplied them with food and materials. Carpenters made tools and built sleds to haul heavy loads. Metal workers created cutting tools and kept them sharp. Potters formed pots used to prepare food and carry water. Bakers were needed to bake bread for the workers. All these people worked together to build the world's first skyscrapers.

1. Pyramids were built mostly from limestone. The stone was dug out of a quarry, or large open pit. Each block of stone weighed several tons.

2. Before construction began, the base of the pyramid was measured off and sand was removed from the site. A platform, built out of limestone, served as the pyramid's foundation.

3. Groups of men hauled the blocks from the quarry to the pyramid site. They used ropes and levers made of wood to lift the blocks onto heavy sleds. If the quarry was far from the pyramid, workers or oxen would pull the sleds to the Nile River. There, barges would carry the blocks to the building site.

Humans are builders. Over thousands of years, people have created ever larger, more amazing structures. From tombs to canals, these engineering wonders continue to amaze us.

6. Workers placed a capstone, a small pyramid-shaped stone, at the top of the pyramid. It may have been covered with gold or another shiny metal to reflect the rays of the sun.

5. The central core of the pyramid was made of stones that formed steps. The space between the steps was filled in by small soft stones. A layer of fine limestone rock was placed against the small stones to make the outside of the pyramid smooth. This outer layer was removed centuries ago, and the stone was used to build Cairo.

Making a Point!

Egypt wasn't the only nation to build pyramids. The shape proved popular with some ancient civilizations.

Mexico

The Pyramid of the Sun is located not far from Mexico City. The vast structure was built by an ancient people of Mexico called the Teotihuacanos (tay-oh-tee-wha-*cahn*-oz) nearly 2,000 years ago. At 246 feet tall and 733 feet wide on each side, it is the third largest pyramid in the world.

India

There are many Hindu temples shaped like pyramids in India. One, the **Brihadeeswara Temple** in Thanjavur, was built in the 11th century. Made of granite, the temple tower is 216 feet high.

4. Blocks were hauled up ramps onto the pyramid. There may have been a single long ramp or many smaller ones. Ramps may have zigzagged up the sides of the pyramid or gone straight up each side. No one knows for sure.

HOW Was Mount Rushmore Built?

The four heads carved on Mount Rushmore, located in the Black Hills of South Dakota, are big shots in every way. The heads of Presidents George Washington, Thomas Jefferson, Theodore Roosevelt, and Abraham Lincoln are each 60 feet tall. Their features are huge: Each nose is 20 feet long, the mouths are 18 feet wide, and each eye is 11 feet across. If their bodies were built to scale, they would be 46 stories high.

During the summer, more than 20,000 visitors come each day to admire the humongous monument. Sculptor Gutzon Borglum began the project in 1927, and it was completed in 1941. During that time, 450,000 tons of granite, a type of stone, was removed from Mount Rushmore, mostly by dynamite. Those explosives helped create one of the largest works of art in the world.

1. Mount Rushmore was picked because the rock could be easily carved. Also, the mountainside received a lot of sunlight, so visitors could view it for most of the day.

6. As Mount Rushmore neared completion in 1941, workers used hammers and chisels to smooth the rock faces.

Borglum's Model on Jefferson & Linco...

2. Borglum made a small model of the four Presidents. Each inch on the model represented one foot on the mountain. Workers used the model to create the sculpture on the mountain.

3. A worker prepares dynamite charges. The dynamite removed rock to within three or four inches of the finished faces, creating the shape of lips, cheeks, noses, necks, and brows.

4. Men worked on the side of the mountain while sitting in leather seats attached to steel cables. Hand-cranked winches raised and lowered the workers.

5. Near the final stages, drillers made many small holes in the granite. The granite between the holes was then wedged off, exposing the final layer of rock.

HOW Does the Panama Canal Work?

Atlantic Ocean

Panama

Pacific Ocean

The Panama Canal is one big ditch. This 300-foot-wide, 51-mile-long gash cutting through the nation of Panama, in Central America, connects the Atlantic and Pacific Oceans. Before the canal was completed in 1914, ships had to travel around the tip of South America to go from New York to San Francisco. The Panama Canal cuts that trip by 8,000 miles.

Most of the Panama Canal is above sea level. So ships that pass through it must be raised and lowered by a series of devices called locks. Today, about 14,000 ships sail through the Panama Canal each year. Some modern ships are too wide to fit in the canal. Panama is hoping to fix the canal so supertankers and other hefty vessels can squeeze through it.

1. A ship that enters the Panama Canal from the Atlantic Ocean begins its journey at Limon Bay.

Atlantic Ocean

3. The water that pours into the Panama Canal's locks flows from Gatun Lake through special pipes. The ship is at its highest point as it sails about 23 miles on the lake.

2. The ship sails at sea level for 6.5 miles to the Gatun locks. There, three separate chambers raise the ship about 85 feet. Now the ship is at the level of Gatun Lake.

4. From Gatun Lake the ship enters the Gaillard Cut, an eight-mile-long channel.

How a Lock Works

When a ship is raised in a canal, it enters a lock. Locks are giant compartments made of thick concrete walls with huge metal doors at each end. One door opens for the ship to enter and closes behind it. Water flows into the compartment, and the ship rises with it. The water continues to flood the lock until it is at the same level as the higher lock ahead of it. Then the front door opens and the ship sails through it into the next lock. Each lock lifts the ship higher and higher. Ships are lowered in locks, too. When a ship enters a lock, the water is pumped out until the ship is at a lower level. Other locks lower the ship more and more.

Miraflores Lake

Pacific Ocean

FACTOID

The Panama Canal was a great—but difficult—building feat. Blasting away rock with dynamite was dangerous. There were accidents with trains carrying equipment. Sometimes the sides of the canal would cave in, burying weeks of work in seconds. And mosquitoes spread deadly diseases among workers. No wonder it took 10 years to complete!

5. At the end of the Gaillard Cut, the ship enters the Pedro Miguel lock. The lock lowers the ship about 30 feet into Miraflores Lake.

6. A two-mile-long channel leads the ship to the two Miraflores locks. They lower the ship to sea level. It takes about seven minutes for water to enter or drain from the locks. The ship sails seven miles until it reaches the Pacific Ocean.

HOW Was a Bridge Built Across the Colorado River?

Engineers develop and design structures and solve problems. They are used to challenges, but this was a tough one: how to span the wide canyon between Nevada and Arizona, nearly 900 feet above the Colorado River. The answer: Build a 1,900-foot-long arch bridge.

The Mike O'Callaghan–Pat Tillman Memorial Bridge took five years to build before it opened in 2010. It is the longest and highest concrete arch bridge in the Western Hemisphere. To build it, engineers first had to measure the height and width of the canyon and the steepness of its walls. Next, they had to choose the best bridge design for the site. An arch bridge was picked because it is the best way to cross a steep canyon. The builders faced another challenge thanks to Hoover Dam, the bridge's neighbor. The engineers felt a special responsibility building a large structure next to an engineering marvel. Most people think they succeeded and produced their own engineering marvel.

The bridge has two side-by-side arches made of steel and concrete. The arches were put together in 52 pieces, half on each side of the canyon. Each piece was 24 feet long.

Each half of the arches was built over the river, and they met in the center. Dozens of temporary cables held up the arches as the bridge grew longer and longer above the river. The cables were attached to temporary towers 155 feet in height.

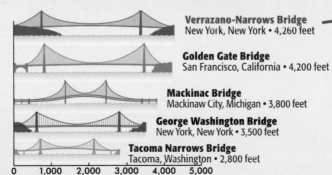

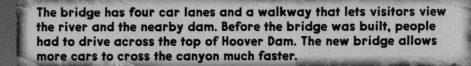

The bridge has four car lanes and a walkway that lets visitors view the river and the nearby dam. Before the bridge was built, people had to drive across the top of Hoover Dam. The new bridge allows more cars to cross the canyon much faster.

The final step was to build a road deck over the arches. It is made of concrete poured over 36 steel girders, each weighing 50 tons.

Large columns are built into the rocks on either side of the river. They help hold up the roadway approaches to the bridge.

 TFK TOP 5 Longest U.S. Suspension Bridges

Many long bridges are suspension bridges. The roadway is held up by wire ropes that stretch from tall towers to the road.

Verrazano-Narrows Bridge
New York, New York • 4,260 feet

Golden Gate Bridge
San Francisco, California • 4,200 feet

Mackinac Bridge
Mackinaw City, Michigan • 3,800 feet

George Washington Bridge
New York, New York • 3,500 feet

Tacoma Narrows Bridge
Tacoma, Washington • 2,800 feet

0   1,000   2,000   3,000   4,000   5,000
feet

HOW to Build a Spaghetti Bridge

Modern bridges are impressive metal structures, but a bridge can be as simple as a log that falls across a stream. Over the centuries, many materials have been used to span water, valleys, or roads, including wood, ropes, and a tough plant called bamboo.

Stone bridges have been constructed for thousands of years—and they can last just as long. Hundreds of stone bridges built by the ancient Romans are still found in many countries. In the 1700s, iron was first used in a bridge. Later, concrete and steel became favorite materials of bridge builders. One material bridge builders don't use is spaghetti. But you can build a pasta bridge—just don't try to eat it!

FACTOID

The spaghetti bridge world record was set by two college students from Hungary. They built a bridge that weighed about 2 pounds and held a weight of 1,257 pounds.

What You Need

- 8 marshmallows
- 3 strands of uncooked linguini
- 14 strands of uncooked spaghetti (try to use spaghetti that's about the same diameter as the linguini)
- 1 paper clip
- 1 envelope
- Scissors
- 40 coins

What to Do

1 Use the scissors to snip off one corner of the envelope. This will be a coin basket.

2 Unbend one end of the paper clip. Poke it through the top of the envelope and bend it into a hook shape so it holds the coin basket.

3 Make two pyramids of equal size by sticking the spaghetti through the marshmallows. Each pyramid will need four marshmallows and six strands of spaghetti.

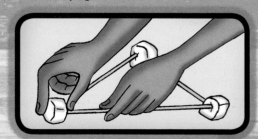

4 Stand up the two pyramids near each other so they are less than the length of a spaghetti strand apart.

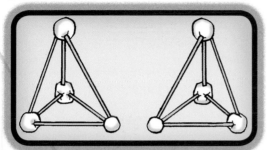

5 Connect one end of a strand of spaghetti to the marshmallow at the top of one pyramid. Connect the other end to the marshmallow atop the other pyramid. This is the bridge.

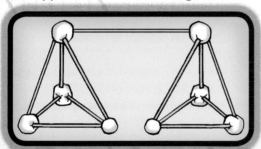

6 Hang the coin basket in the middle of the bridge. Add coins one by one to the basket until the spaghetti bridge breaks. Note how many coins it took to break the bridge.

7 Connect the two pyramids with a strand of linguini. Repeat the experiment. Note the difference in the number of coins it took to make each bridge collapse.

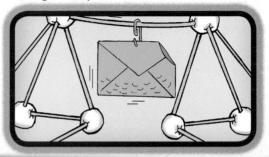

What Happened

Two strong shapes held up the bridge: triangles and circles. The spaghetti pyramids are made of triangles. Triangles are strong because they are rigid and won't bend. Spaghetti is shaped like a cylinder, and round objects have great strength. Stress is distributed equally throughout them, and they will bend in any direction. Rectangles bend in one direction. The linguini is shaped like a rectangle and so it bends and breaks.

FACTOID

Kelowna, Canada, is famous for its Spaghetti Bridge contest held at Okanagan College. Each year, students compete to build the strongest bridges out of dry noodles. This spaghetti bridge, built by James Dessert, took first place in 2014. It held about 248 pounds before it bent.

HOW to Build a Pyramid

Pyramids have fascinated builders for thousands of years. Not only does a pyramid have a cool shape, but it is also very stable. Because it has much more weight on the bottom than the top, it won't topple. That's why cheerleaders and circus acrobats enjoy making human pyramids.

The outside surfaces of a pyramid slant up to meet at a point, called the apex. A pyramid can be built with different numbers of sides. A three-sided pyramid has a triangle-shaped base, so it is called a triangular pyramid. A pyramid with four sides has a four-sided base. It is called a square pyramid. The base of the pyramid with five sides is a pentagonal, or five-sided, pyramid, and so on. It took workers 20 years to build the Great Pyramid, in Giza, Egypt. But you can build a great pyramid in less than an hour.

FACTOID

The entrance to the Louvre Museum in Paris, France, is a 70-foot-high metal and glass pyramid surrounded by three smaller pyramids.

What You Need

- Small block or other square object to use as a pattern, about two or three inches on a side. You can use a larger block to make a larger pyramid. In that case, you might also need larger paper.
- Stiff sheet of paper, about 8½ inches by 11 inches or larger
- A piece of paper a little larger than the block
- Pen or pencil
- Scissors
- Glue
- Ruler or triangle

What to Do

1 Place the square block over the smaller paper and trace the block's four sides with the pen. You should have drawn a perfect square. This square is the pattern square. Place the block in the center of the larger paper and trace it again. This is the base square.

2 Cut out the pattern square with scissors. Then fold the square in half. Open it up and fold it again the other way, so the pattern square has been divided into quarters.

3 Make a dot with the pen at each fold on the edge of the square.

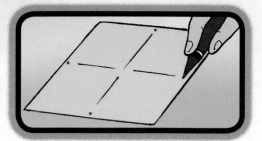

4 Place the pattern square on top of the base square, so the sides line up. Use the pattern square to mark the center point of each side on the base square: The dots on the pattern sqaure will be at the center points.

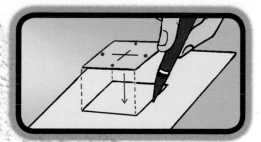

5 Lay the pattern square on the larger paper as shown, with one corner of the pattern square touching a dot on the base square. Make a dot on the larger paper at the opposite point of the pattern square. The dot should line up with the opposite center points of the pattern square.

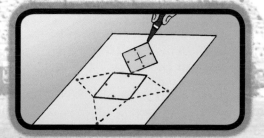

6 Draw straight lines connecting the dots on the larger paper to the corners of the base square. You can use a ruler. It should end up looking like a four-pointed star, or four triangles with a box at the center. Draw a small tab or flap on the same side of each triangle, as shown.

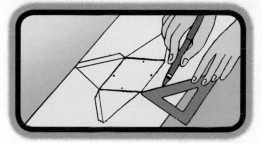

7 Use the scissors to cut along the outermost lines of the larger paper. Fold the four triangles and tabs in toward the box, so they meet to form a pyramid. They should fit together. Unfold them. Fold and unfold the tabs.

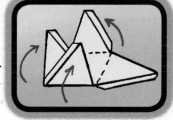

8 Glue each tab and press it against the inside of the adjoining triangle. If you have trouble sticking them to the insides of the triangles, stick them to the outsides. Decorate your pyramid to make it look like an Egyptian pyramid. Or coat the pyramid in glue and sprinkle it with sand so it has a desert look.

HOW Do Submarines Work?

Submarines do one thing that regular ships don't want to do: They sink. A sub has an outside hull and an inside hull. Between the two hulls are compartments called ballast tanks. When the tanks are filled with seawater, the sub is heavier than water. It sinks. When air is pumped into the ballast tanks to force out all the water, the sub is lighter than water. It rises.

Subs have been used to explore the depths of the oceans. They are also big weapons of war. Submarines played a major part in World War I and World War II. Today, nuclear-powered submarines packed with missiles patrol the seas. Subs are an amazing form of transportation—if you don't mind being in a tight squeeze.

Rudders: Steer subs left and right.

Propeller shaft: Turns propeller.

Maneuvering room: Controls the nuclear reactor.

Propeller: Moves ship forward.

Ballast tanks: Fill and empty with water so sub can rise and sink.

Engine: Steam turns generator, which turns the propeller shaft. Steam also turns turbine generator, which provides electricity to the sub.

Nuclear reactor: Produces heat to change water into steam.

Cars, trains, and planes make it a snap to travel just about anywhere. And new technologies promise that we'll be getting around faster and more efficiently than ever before.

Bridge: Holds periscope, radio antennas, radar, and other electronic sensors.

Sonar room: Sonar bounces sounds off objects outside the sub. The echoes let the crew stationed here know what's out there—friends or enemies—and how far away they are.

Torpedoes and torpedo tubes

Control room and attack center: Contains systems and crew to steer ship. The orders to launch torpedoes and missiles are delivered from here.

Officers' cabin: Officers sleep here.

Sonar dome: Contains hundreds of sound detectors.

Crew's mess: Dining room

Crew bunks: Crew sleeps here.

HOW Does a Hybrid Car Work?

The United States is a nation of automobiles. In fact, there are about 245 million of them on American roads. But cars have two big problems: They cause pollution and they run on costly gas. One solution that carmakers have come up with is the hybrid car. A hybrid car is a combination of two power sources—gas and electricity.

Hybrid cars save on fuel. One reason is that they run mostly on electricity provided by batteries. And because hybrids usually are smaller and lighter than normal cars, they need less power to run. Hybrid cars are not as polluting as gas guzzlers. Electricity doesn't give off any pollution, and hybrids burn less gas and do it more efficiently than regular cars.

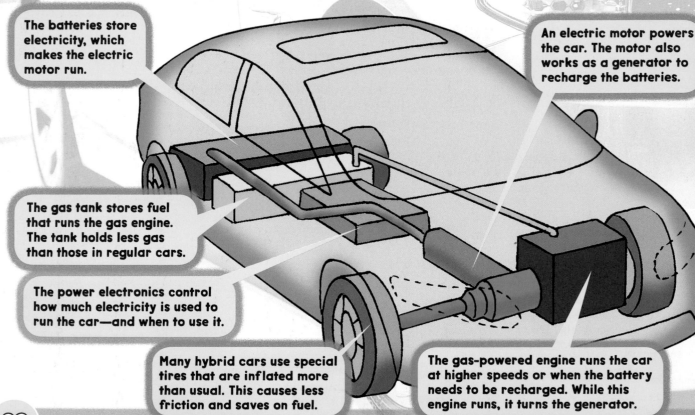

The batteries store electricity, which makes the electric motor run.

An electric motor powers the car. The motor also works as a generator to recharge the batteries.

The gas tank stores fuel that runs the gas engine. The tank holds less gas than those in regular cars.

The power electronics control how much electricity is used to run the car—and when to use it.

Many hybrid cars use special tires that are inflated more than usual. This causes less friction and saves on fuel.

The gas-powered engine runs the car at higher speeds or when the battery needs to be recharged. While this engine runs, it turns the generator.

A hybrid car is made of lightweight materials to help increase mileage. The shape of a car's body is designed so that it has less resistance to wind so it uses less fuel.

Hybrid vs. Electric

A hybrid car runs on both an electric motor and a gas-powered motor. The hybrid uses the electric motor to travel at slow speeds. When the car goes at higher speeds, the gas engine turns on automatically. If more power is needed, the electric motor and gas motor can work at the same time. If the batteries run low, the gas engine will take over and recharge the batteries as the car runs.

An electric car is powered only by electricity. It needs more batteries than a hybrid, often 12 to 24 of them. The batteries must be recharged about every 100 miles. They can be recharged by plugging them in at home in a wall outlet for a few hours. Charging stations, like the one in the photo below, also provide electricity for recharging batteries.

A High-Flying Car

The Terrafugia Transition® is a really unusual hybrid. The amazing vehicle is both a car and an airplane. The $279,000 personal aircraft gets 35 miles per gallon on the road and comes with airbags and a full vehicle parachute. On the ground, its wings are folded up. When the wings come down at an airport, it can fly two passengers about 410 miles at a speed of 100 miles per hour. With this vehicle, you need both a driver's and a pilot's license.

HOW Are Tunnels Dug?

Tunnels can be dug through miles of mountains or under cities. Mammoth-sized machinery is used to dig the huge holes. The machine that most large projects use is called a tunnel-boring machine (TBM). It has a giant spinning disc that cuts through solid rock. TBMs were used to cut through mountains in the Alps to create the longest tunnel ever built—the Gotthard Base Tunnel, which links Switzerland and Italy in Europe. The train tunnel is slightly more than 35 miles long!

1. The front of some TBMs have shields to keep pieces of rock from falling down and burying the machine.

Sometimes when transportation tunnels are dug, two tunnels are built side by side so cars or trains can travel in both directions. Most tunnels are dug from the opposite ends and meet in the middle.

The TBMs for the Gotthard tunnel each weighed about 6 million pounds and were 1,300 feet long. They dug 96 feet of tunnel a week. It takes 20 to 25 people to operate a TBM.

Longest Railroad Tunnels

TUNNEL	LOCATION	LENGTH IN MILES	OPENED
1. Gotthard Base	Switzerland-Italy	35.4	Completed 2010. Not open until 2017
2. Seikan	Japan	33.5	1988
3. Channel	England-France	31.1	1994
4. Lotschberg Base	Switzerland	21.5	2007
5. Guadarrama	Spain	17.6	2007

Source: World Book

5. An elevator carries dug-up rock to the surface. The rock may be placed in a landfill or used in another project, such as a road. At Gotthard, some rock was used to make the concrete that covered the tunnel walls.

How a Tunnel Is Built

Surface

3. Crumbled rock is carried to the back of the TBM by a conveyor belt. The rock drops into a cart and is removed from the area.

Concrete sections to line the tunnel are lowered down a shaft.

2. The rotating cutters of the TBM can be 50 feet in diameter. Their super-strong titanium teeth rotate slowly, breaking up the rock as the TBM moves forward.

4. The walls of a finished tunnel are usually lined with steel or concrete or a combination of both materials. The Gotthard tunnel walls are made of concrete and a special steel that won't break under the great pressure of the Alps.

FACTOID

Enough material was removed from the Gotthard Base Tunnel to fill the Empire State Building 13 times.

HOW Does a Maglev Train Work?

A levitating train floats in the air—but it's not a magic trick. Maglev is short for "magnetic levitation," and maglev trains use the push and pull of magnetism to travel above their tracks. The opposite poles of a magnet attract each other. That attraction allows one kind of maglev train to levitate. The same poles of a magnet repel each other, which is why another kind of maglev train can float. With no friction from wheels to slow them down, these magnetic marvels can reach speeds of more than 300 miles per hour. Even the fastest American trains don't go faster than 80 miles per hour.

Today, maglev trains are running full-time only in China. But maglev trains are being tested in Germany and Japan. They may one day come to the United States. When that happens, people who love riding trains will really be floating on air!

Maglev trains ride above and inside the guideway.

The bottom of the train contains powerful magnets.

One type of maglev train lifts up before it moves forward and doesn't ride on the tracks. The other type rides on wheels at low speeds until the magnetism is strong enough to make it float.

Fastest Trains

The fastest trains normally go at speeds of around 200 miles per hour. But some can travel much faster. These are the top speeds reached by passenger trains during test runs.

TRAIN	COUNTRY	TYPE OF TRAIN	SPEED (MILES PER HOUR)	DATE
1. JP-Maglev	Japan	maglev	361	2003
2. TGV	France	standard	357	2007
3. Shinkansen MLX01	Japan	maglev	320	1990
4. Shanghai Transrapid	China	maglev	311	2003
5. TR-07	Germany	maglev	270	1989

Source: Forbes.com/Zimbio.com

Shinkansen MLX01

Shanghai Maglev

Electricity sent through wires in the guideway creates an electromagnetic field. The magnetism attracts or repels the maglev's magnets (depending on the type of train), lifting the cars as much as three inches.

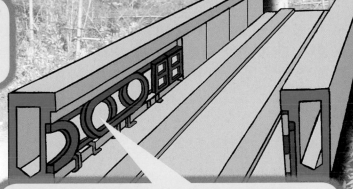

Current in coils along the guideway constantly changes direction, reversing its magnetic field. The magnetism pulls the front of the train and pushes the back of the train. This makes the train go forward.

HOW Does a Toilet Flush Away Waste?

Getting rid of poop can be a problem. The earliest form of waste disposal was a pit in the ground. In ancient India, some cities had toilets that drained waste into underground chambers. The toilets of early Romans dropped waste into running water that carried it away. In Europe during the Middle Ages, many people deposited their waste in bowls, called chamber pots. People sometimes threw the contents of the pots out the window and into the street, where it flowed into open drains.

It wasn't until 1596 that the first flush toilet was invented, by Englishman Sir John Harrington. Over the following centuries, advances were made in toilet technology—as well as in toilet-related products. For example, in 1857, Joseph Gayetty came up with the idea of selling toilet paper in a package. The Scott Paper Company started selling toilet paper on a roll in 1879.

By the early 1900s, the modern toilet had been developed, and today it may be the most important seat in the house.

FACTOID

The most expensive toilet on Earth isn't on Earth. It's the one used by astronauts on the International Space Station. Each toilet costs $19 million.

1. A tank can hold several gallons of water.

5. As the tank empties, the float sinks. When the float reaches the bottom of the tank, it opens a valve, sending water into the tank. As the tank fills, the float rises. At the top of the tank, the float shuts the valve, cutting off the water. Now you can flush again.

4. After the bowl fills with water, the siphon sucks everything into a pipe that leads to the sewer system.

2. When the handle is pressed, a chain lifts a flap.

3. The flap covers a hole at the bottom of the tank. When the flap lifts up, all the water in the tank pours into the bowl. When the tank is empty, the flap closes.

Waste Not...

Most toilets whoosh down several gallons of water every time they flush. Toilets account for 25 percent of all water used in a house. To save water, new types of toilets have been invented.

○ **Old toilets** use 3 to 5 gallons a flush. Newer toilets are able to flush while only using 1.6 gallons. That can save the average home 100 gallons a day.

○ **Dual flush toilets** allow users to flush two different ways. Press one button for solid waste and the toilet uses 1.6 gallons. For liquid waste, it flushes 0.79 gallons.

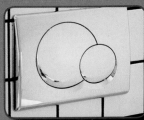

○ **Composting toilets** use almost no water. The waste goes into a container that changes it into useable compost. Compost is made when bacteria break down natural substances. Owners of a composting toilet might have to add air, worms, or bacteria to the container to help the waste become safe compost. Fans remove any smells in the bathroom through a pipe that leads outside.

FACTOID

Among the many names for toilet are latrine, water closet, privy, lavatory, throne, chamber pot, commode, and john.

HOW to Make a Baking-Soda Boat

When submarines and other seagoing craft move forward in the water, they're applying a law discovered by the famous scientist Sir Isaac Newton. His third law of motion states that for every action there is an equal and opposite reaction. In other words, if you push an object in one direction, a force pushes you in the opposite direction. With engine-powered ships, the push comes from a propeller.

A propeller pushes water backward and the opposite reaction moves the ship forward. You don't need propellers to push water backward. Rowers do it using oars. Swimmers do it with their arms. You can apply Newton's third law of motion yourself by making a boat fueled with baking soda and vinegar.

What You Need

- A wading pool or bathtub filled with water
- Vinegar
- Baking soda
- Toilet paper
- 12-ounce plastic soda bottle with cap
- Thumbtack or push pin (optional)
- Measuring spoon and measuring cup
- A few marbles or pebbles

What to Do

1 Wash out the soda bottle so it's clean and dry inside.

2 Lay out four squares of connected toilet paper so they're flat. Fold the toilet paper in half.

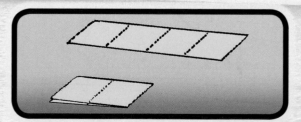

3 Put one or two tablespoons of baking soda on the two connected toilet paper squares and spread out the powder. Then roll up the toilet paper tightly so the baking soda can't leak out. You can twist the ends of the toilet paper to close them.

4 Add some marbles or pebbles to the bottle so it will sink partway down in the water. Place the rolled-up toilet paper in the soda bottle.

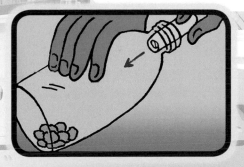

5 If you have a thumbtack or push pin, use it to make several small holes in the cap. Keep the soda bottle cap handy. Or have a friend hold it. Pour one-quarter cup of vinegar into the bottle.

6 If you made holes in the cap, screw it on the bottle quickly and tightly. If you didn't make holes, place the cap on the bottle loosely, giving it only one twist.

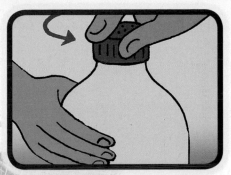

7 Shake the bottle to mix the vinegar and baking soda. Place the bottle in the pool or bathtub. Anchors aweigh!

What Happened

The boat is powered by a gas you can't see. When the baking soda and vinegar combine, they form carbon dioxide. The gas fills the bottle and escapes through the openings in the cap. The gas pushes against the water, causing the boat to move forward. Newton's third law works every time!

HOW to Make a Paper Airplane

People have been making objects out of paper for centuries in China, Germany, Spain, and other countries. In Japan, the art of folding paper is called origami (or-eh-*gahm*-ee). Origami experts can make almost anything out of a piece of paper—from a hang glider to a beetle to a racing car. Here's how you can fold a sheet of paper into an airplane that flies. It's an uplifting experience.

FACTOIDS

- In 2004, NASA's X-43A set the speed record as the fastest ever jet-powered aircraft. For 10 seconds, the unpiloted test craft traveled at Mach 9.6, or more than nine times the speed of sound. That's 7,000 miles per hour!

- Takuo Toda, an engineer and chairman of the Japan Origami Airplane Association, says the best way to keep a paper airplane aloft is to throw it straight up in the air.

What You Need

- A sheet of paper 8½ inches by 11 inches. The paper can be smaller or bigger, but it should be rectangular.

What to Do

1 Take the sheet of paper and fold it in half the long way. Then open the paper so there is a crease down the middle.

2 Take one end of the paper and fold in one of the two corners. The inside of the corner fold should line up with the center crease. Do the same with the other corner.

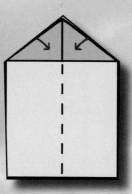

3 Fold each outer corner so it lines up with the center crease.

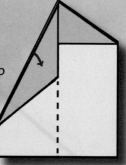

4 Fold along the main crease so you can see the body of the airplane.

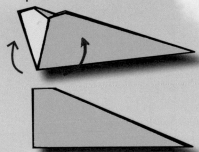

5 Fold one wing down so its edge lines up with the center crease. Repeat with the other wing.

6 Unfold the wings so your plane is ready for takeoff. Throw it like a dart to make it fly. If it crashes too quickly, adjust the wings.

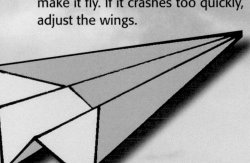

Strangest Airplanes

Check out these weird aircraft. They are just "plane" crazy!

1. VZ-9AV Avrocar It looks like a flying saucer or a giant hubcap. Its biggest problem? Anytime it flew higher than three feet, it wobbled like Jell-O.

2. H-4 Hercules (Spruce Goose) At 320 feet from the tip of one wing to the tip of the other, the Spruce Goose's wingspan was longer than a football field. Its body was made of laminated wood glued together.

3. Martin Marietta X-24 Something seems missing from this little jet—its wings! The Air Force built it to test how a spacecraft might act when reentering Earth's atmosphere. Even wingless, the plane went 1,036 miles per hour.

4. Vought V-173 (Flying Pancake) This flat plane was made of wood and fabric—and, no, it didn't run on syrup. The plane just didn't stack up, so now it sits in the Smithsonian Institution's Air and Space Museum.

5. Zveno Bomber Fighter This plane was double trouble! In the 1920s, the Soviet Air Force built a giant bomber that carried small fighter planes attached to the wings above and below the main body of the bomber. If the "mother ship" was attacked, the fighters would launch like angry bees to protect it.

Glossary

antenna a metal device used for sending and receiving radio waves
asteroid rocks, some the size of small planets, that orbit between Mars and Jupiter
axis a straight line around which an object turns

bacteria microscopic single-celled organisms found in water, air, and soil
baking soda a substance that gives off carbon dioxide, which causes dough to rise
battery a device that produces an electrical current
buoyancy the ability of an object to float or rise when submerged in a liquid

canal a human-made waterway used for travel, to ship goods, or to irrigate land
canyon a deep valley with steep sides, often formed by a river
centrifugal force the force directed away from the center of a revolving body
comet a large chunk of rock surrounded by frozen gas and ice that orbits the sun
constellation a group of stars that seem to form a pattern in the sky

electromagnetic field a magnetic field produced when electricity flows through a wire
electron a tiny particle that moves around the nucleus of an atom
exoplanet a planet outside our solar system

friction the force that one surface exerts on another when the two rub against each other

generator a machine that changes mechanical energy into electrical energy, often by moving a copper wire through a magnetic field
glacier a large mass of ice and snow that has been pressed down over thousands of years and which slowly moves forward
gravity the force of attraction between two objects

hybrid something that combines two or more different things, such as a car that runs on electricity and gas

kinetic energy the energy of movement

landfill a site designed so large amounts of trash can be buried safely
limestone a kind of rock often used as a building material
liquid hydrogen hydrogen gas that has been cooled down into a liquid; it is used as rocket fuel
lock a large chamber with gates at each end that fills with water to raise ships and empties water to lower ships as they pass through it

magnetic field the lines of force created by and surrounding the sun and the planets

magnet an object that attracts or repels other magnets and attracts certain kinds of metal, such as iron and nickel

magnetosphere the magnetic field that surrounds a planet and which extends far into outer space

molecule the smallest part of a substance, made up of one or more atoms

nuclear reactor a device that uses radioactive materials to produce heat, which generates electrical power

orbit the path one body takes around another, such as the path of the Earth around the sun

pentagonal a shape that has five sides and five angles inside the shape

pharaoh a king of ancient Egypt

photon a small particle of energy that all forms of electromagnetic radiation are made of

pollution the contamination of air, water, or soil by harmful substances

potential energy stored energy

propeller spinning blades that make a boat, submarine, or airplane move

quarry an open area from which stones used for building things, such as limestone, are removed

radiation electromagnetic energy that moves in the form of waves

solar panel a device made up of solar cells, which change sunlight into electricity

sonar a method or device that locates objects by sending out sound waves and detecting the waves that bounce off the objects

suspension bridge a bridge whose roadway is suspended by cables attached to large towers at both ends

ultraviolet radiation electromagnetic waves invisible to the human eye that can damage human cells

vapor a gas; also, tiny but visible particles that float in the air, such as smoke and steam

Credits

All illustrations and diagrams by Felipe Galindo unless indicated otherwise.

Cover: Mark Wainwright/Symbology Creative (background); Markus Gann/Shutterstock.com (sun); Lightspring/Shutterstock.com (Earth top right); pixbox77/Shutterstock.com (stars); Fer Gregory/Shutterstock.com (space shuttle); Henrik Lehnerer/Shutterstock.com (astronaut); Johan Swanepoel/Shutterstock.com (Earth bottom).

Back cover: Mark Wainwright/Symbology Creative (background); ©3DSculptor/iStock/Thinkstock (spacecraft); jupeart/Shutterstock.com (stars top right); ©artlensfoto/iStock/Thinkstock (sunglasses); ©Martin Adams/iStock/Thinkstock (Jupiter); ©Pitris iStock/Thinkstock (stars bottom right); Mark Wainwright/Symbology Creative (book covers).

Interior: 1: Mark Wainwright/Symbology Creative (background); Henrik Lehnerer/Shutterstock.com (astronaut); Johan Swanepoel/Shutterstock.com (Earth). 2–3: Zhana Ocheret/Shutterstock.com (background). 3: Tim the Finn/Shutterstock.com (space rocks); Pius Lee/Shutterstock.com (pyramid).4–5: jules2000/Shutterstock.com (background); Tim the Finn/Shutterstock.com (space rocks). 5: Sovfoto/UIG via Getty Images (Tunguska). 6–7: NASA/JPL-Caltech (background). 6: NASA/JPL-Caltech/LMSS (building juno). 7: NASA/JPL (clouds); NASA/JPL/Johns Hopkins University Applied Physics Laboratory (magnetic field); fluidworkshop/Shutterstock.com (solar system). 8–9: Mack7777/Shutterstock.com (background). 8: NASA (all). 9: NASA (all). 10–11: ©iStockPhoto.com/adventtr (background). 11: ©iStockPhoto.com/o-che (sunscreen). 12–13: ©iStockPhoto.com (background). 14–15: Ken Freeman/Shutterstock.com (background). 14: Library of Congress, Prints and Photographs Division (orrery). 15: eddtoro/Shutterstock.com (Hayden Sphere). 16–17: Jose Antonio Perez/Shutterstock.com (background). 18–19: R-O-M-A/Shutterstock.com (background); Pius Lee/Shutterstock.com (pyramid). 18: Brian Maudsley/Shutterstock.com (limestone bricks); Victor V. Hoguns Zhugin/Shutterstock.

com (top of pyramid). 19: Marcos Carvalho/Shutterstock.com (Pyramid of the Sun); Raj Krish/Shutterstock.com (Brihadeeswara Temple). 20–21: KJ2495/Shutterstock.com (background). 20: Photo courtesy of U.S. National Park Service (all). 21: Library of Congress, Prints and Photographs Division (model); Photo courtesy of U.S. National Park Service (worker with dynamite, workers on seats, drilling holes). 22–23: B. Franklin/Shutterstock.com (background). 22: Globe Turner/Shutterstock.com (map). 23: Chris Jenner/Shutterstock.com (canal locks); Library of Congress, Prints and Photographs Division (canal factoid). 24–25: ©Spaces Images/SuperStock (background). 25: Photo by K. Oliver (completed bridge); Stephen Blue for TIME For Kids (bridge illustrations); JaysonPhotography/Shutterstock.com (Verrazano-Narrows Bridge). 26–27: Jeff Banke/Shutterstock.com (background). 27: Courtesy of KelownaNow.com (James Dessert). 28–29: R-O-M-A/Shutterstock.com (background). 28: tungtopgun/Shutterstock.com (Louvre). 30–31: Sergey Orlov/Shutterstock.com (back). 31: U.S. Navy Photo (Nautilus). 32–33: Jordan Tan/Shutterstock.com (background); Darren Brode/Shutterstock.com (car). 33: Sopotnicki/Shutterstock.com (charging cars); Courtesy of Terrafugia (all Terrafugia Transition images). 34–35: evan66/Shutterstock.com (background). 34: evan66/Shutterstock.com (two tunnels); AP Photo/Christian Hartmann, Pool (tunnel boring machine). 36–37: mamahoohooba/Shutterstock.com (background); Courtesy of Transrapid (maglev train). 36: Courtesy of Transrapid (train magnets). 37: ©Sakuragirin/Dreamstime.com (Shinkansen MLX01); Lee Prince/Shutterstock.com (Shanghai Maglev). 38–39: Africa Studio/Shutterstock.com (background). 39: Einar Muoni/Shutterstock.com (toilet); Hadrian/Shutterstock.com (dual flush). 40–41: Ruth Peterkin/Shutterstock.com (background). 42–43: Vera Volkova/Shutterstock.com (background). 43: U.S. Air Force Photo (VZ-9AV Avrocar); NASA (Martin Marietta X-24); U.S. Navy Photo 44–45: Zhanna Ocheret/Shutterstock.com. 46: Guilu/Shutterstock.com. 47–48: Zhanna Ocheret/Shutterstock.com.

A

airplanes
    in astronaut training, 8
    how to make a paper, 42-43
    jet-powered, 42
    strangest, 43
Alps, 34
Arizona, 24
asteroids
    locating and tracking, 4
    nuclear blasts, 5
    striking Earth, 4
astronauts
    in rockets, 16
    in simulators, 9
    in zero gravity conditions, 8-9
    mission specialists, 8
    requirements to become, 8
    training, 8-9
Atlantic Ocean, 22

B

baking soda boat
    how to make, 40-41
ballast tanks, 30
batteries, 32-33
Borglum, Gutzon, 20
bridge
    George Washington, 25
    Golden Gate, 25
    how to build a spaghetti bridge, 24-25
    Mackinac, 25
    Mike O'Callaghan-Pat Tillman
        Memorial, 23-24
    Tacoma Narrows, 25
    types of, 26
    Verrazano-Narrows, 25
Brihadeeswara Temple, 19

C

Cairo, 18, 19
California, 25
capstone, 19
car
    electric, 33
    hybrid, 32-33
carbon dioxide
    in baking soda and vinegar, 41

Central America, 22
Channel England-France, 35
China, 37, 42, 16
clouds, 7
Colorado River, 24-25
comets, 4
compost, 39
constellations
    Big Dipper, 15
    in ancient times, 15
    Orion, 15

E

Earth
    and Jupiter, 7
    and the sun, 10, 12
    Earth-like worlds, 12-13
    hit by asteroids, 4
    temperatures, 43
Egypt, 18, 28
electric car
    charging stations, 33
    vs. hybrid, 33
electricity
    in cars, 32-33
    in maglev trains, 37
electromagnetic field
    in Jupiter, 7
    in train guideways, 37
exoplanets
    discovered, 13
    Earth-like life in, 12
    Goldilock region, 12
eyes
    protection against sun, 11

F

fireworks, 16

G

Galliard Cut, 22
Gatun Lake, 22
Gatun locks, 22
Gayetty, Joseph, 38
generator, 32
George Washington Bridge, 25
Germany, 36, 42
Giza, 18, 28
Goddard, Robert, 16
Golden Gate Bridge, 25
Gotthard Base Tunnel, 34-35
Guadarrama Tunnel, 35

H

H-4 Hercules, 43
Harrington, Sir John, 38
Hayden Sphere, 15

helium
    in Jupiter, 7
    in the sun, 10
Hoover Dam, 24-25
Houston, TX, 8
Hungary, 26
hybrid car
    batteries in, 32
    parts of, 32-33
    shape of, 33
    vs. electric, 33
hydrogen
    in the sun, 10
    liquid, 16

I

India, 19, 38
International Space Station (ISS), 38, 8

J

Japan, 35, 37, 42
Japan Origami Airplane Association, 42
Juno probe
    pulling together, 6
    solar panels in, 6
Jupiter
    atmosphere in, 6-7
    bands and belts in, 7
    facts on, 7
    magnetic field in, 7

K

Kelowna, Canada, 27

L

limestone, 18-19
Limon Bay, 22
liquid hydrogen, 16
Lotschberg Base Tunnel, 35
Louvre Museum, 28
Lyndon B. Johnson Space Center, 8

M

Mackinac Bridge, 25
maglev train
    current in coils, 37
    electromagnetic field, 37
    guideway, 36
    how it works, 36-37
    J-P Maglev, 37
    Shanghai Transrapid, 37
    Shinkansen MLX01, 37
    speeds of, 36
    TR-07, 37
Manson, IL, 4
Mars, 12
Martin Marietta X-24, 43

Mercury, 12
Mexico, 19
Mike O'Callahan-Pat Tillman
    Memorial Bridge
    arches in, 24
    Hoover Dam, 25
    how it was built, 24-25
    temporary cables, 24
Milky Way, 14
Miraflores Lake, 23
Mount Rushmore
    Black Hills, 20
    dimension of faces, 20
    presidents portrayed, 20
    tools used in construction, 21

N

NASA Near Earth Collision Program, 4
NASA, 42, 6
Neutral Buoyancy Laboratory, 8
Nevada, 24
New York City, 15
Newton, Sir Isaac
    third law of motion, 40
Nile River, 18
nuclear fusion, 10

O

Oasis of the Sea, 41
Okanagan University, 27
origami, 42
oxygen, 16

P

Pacific Ocean, 23
Panama Canal
    Gaillard Cut, 22
    Gatun Lake, 22
    Gatus locks, 22
    how a lock works, 23
    how it was built, 23
    Limon Bay, 22
    Miraflores Lake, 23
    Miraflores locks, 23
    parts of, 22-23
    Pedro Miguel lock, 23
Panama, 22
Paris, France, 28
pharaohs, 18
planetarium
    first modern, 14
    how to build, 14-15
planets
    Jupiter, 6-7
    Mars, 13
    Mercury, 12

orbiting stars, 12
seen in planetariums, 14
Venus, 12
poop, 38
propeller
    in boats, 40
    in submarines, 30
pyramids
    Brihadeeswara Temple, 19
    Egyptian, 18-19
    how they were built, 18-19
    limestone, 18-19
    Pyramid of the Sun, 19
    ramps, 19
    sides of, 28
    to build a spaghetti bridge, 26
    tools to build, 18-19

R

rivers,
    Colorado, 24
    Nile, 18
rocket
    how to launch, 16-17
    in history, 16
    Robert Goddard, 16
    speed of, 17

S

Seikan Tunnel, 35
skin
    protecting against sun, 11
Smithsonian Institution's Air and
      Space Museum, 43
solar system
    exoplanets, 12
    Jupiter in, 6-7
    planets in our, 12
South America, 22
South Dakota, 20
spacecraft
    around space rocks, 5
    Juno, 6-7
submarines
    as weapons of war, 30
    parts of, 30-31
    USS *Nautilus*, 31
sun
    hydrogen in, 10
    in history, 10
    nuclear fusion, 10
    parts of, 10-11
    Pyramid of the, 19
    safety, 11
    sunscreen, 11
    temperature of, 10

UV rays, 11
Switzerland, 34

T

Tacoma Narrows Bridge, 25
Teotihuacanos, 19
Terrafugia Transition, 33
Toda, Takuo, 42
toilet
    composting, 39
    dual flush, 39
    in history, 38
    invention of flush, 38
    names for, 39
    paper, 38
    parts of, 38-39
    the most expensive, 38
    water-saving, 39
Top 5
    fastest trains, 37
    longest railroad tunnels, 35
    strangest airplanes, 43
Tunguska, Russia, 5
tunnel boring machine (TBM), 34-35
tunnel
    Channel England-France, 35
    Gotthard Base, 34-35
    Guadarrama, 35
    how it is built, 34-35
    Lotschberg Base, 35
    Seikan, 35
    tunnel boring machine (TBM), 34
20,000 Leagues Under the Sea, 31

U

United States
    cars in, 32
    maglev trains in, 36
USS *Nautilus*, 31

V

Venus, 12
Verne, Jules, 31
Verrazano-Narrows Bridge, 25
Vought V-123, 43
VZ-9AV Avrocar, 43

W

weightlessness, 8
wind, 7
World War I and II, 30

X-Y-Z

zero gravity, 8-9
Zveno Bomber Fighter, 43